FOR THE LOVE OF A DOG

A heartwarming gift book for dog owners and dog lovers

By Norisha Taylor

Dogs are not just pets. They are companions, confidants, and family. In their silent gaze, their wagging tails, and their gentle paws, they hold a love that transcends words. This book is a tribute to that bond, the one that speaks not through language, but through every shared glance, every moment of trust. This is the story of the heart of a dog. If you have ever been close to a dog, then let your heart be swept away by the poetic magic of this enchanting tribute.

(1)

The Silent Conversations

We don't need words to understand,
In your shiny eyes, I see love, soft and grand.
When your tail wags, it's all I need to know—
"I'm here, I'm yours,"
you say, in a steady, loving flow.

You feel my moods, my highs and lows,
And with a nudge, you let me know.
No need to speak, no need to try—
In your presence, I can hear
the quiet, comforting sigh.

Paws and Hearts

Your paws on my lap, soft as the breeze,
Each touch, each step, brings me to my knees.
Your rhythm matches mine
at the perfect time,

A heartbeat steady, a love sublime.
You don't need words, no grand display—
In every touch,
you show me the way.

(5)

In the Shiny Eyes of a Dog

When the world is loud
and too much to bear,
I look into your eyes,
and find peace there.

Calm and patient, your gaze is true,
A love without question,
unconditional too.

In your eyes, I find my quiet abode,
A place where
no words are needed to roam.

(7)

Through Every Season

Through every season,
we walk side by side,
From clumsy puppy steps
to the years that glide.

Through coldest winters and summers so bright,
You're there with me, day and night.

No asks, no demands,
just love without end,
Through every moment,
my loyal friend.

(9)

The Gift of Presence

You don't need to speak
to make me whole,
Just your presence,
is enough to heal my soul.

When the world feels
too much to endure, You sit beside me,
and you cure.

No words are needed, only your grace—
In your quiet companionship,
I find my place.

(11)

Forever by My Side

We don't talk of the future,
but I know it's true, You'll be with me,
always, totally and through.

In joy and sorrow, in laughter and tears,
Your love will remain, through all the years.

One day time may take you away,
But in my heart,
you'll forever stay.

(13)

The Echo of Your Heartbeat

There are days when
words just fade,
But your heartbeat,
it never betrays.

In the quiet, I hear it clear,
A steady thrum that draws me near.

Like a song, it soothes my soul,
A rhythm that makes me
feel whole.

The Language of Love

No voice,
no need to speak at all,
Your gestures say it all.

A nudge, a paw on my knee,
A wag that says, "
Stay close to me."

A language forged in trust and care,
A love unspoken,
always there.

(17)

You Make Me Better

You don't just love me—
you shape me too,
Through your patience,
I see what's true.

Your joy reminds me to find the small things,
In your forgiveness, a new beginning springs.

Every day you teach me
to be more, And for that,
I'll love you forevermore.

(19)

A Home Without Words

When I come home,
there's no need to say,
"You missed me,"—
I see it in your gaze.

A wag, a nuzzle, a tail that swings,
And that's all I need—
no other things.

In your presence, I'm home, I'm safe,
I'm found, In your love,
I'm always unbound.

(21)

The Gift of Being With You

There's nothing
more precious, more true,
Than the quiet moments
I share with you.

The walks, the naps, the simple bliss,
In your company,
I find my peace.

Together, we need no grand design,
For in every moment,
your heart beats with mine.

(23)

The Bond That Transcends Time

We may not have forever,
but we have today, And in each now,
we're never far away.

Time may pass, but our love will stay,
In every memory, in every sway.

When I look back, I'll see it clear—
The heart of a dog
is always near.

(25)

You Are My Heart, You Are My Soul

You're more than
just my dog, you're my light,
My joy, my peace, my heart's delight.

In every wag, in every nuzzle close,
You remind me
what truly matters most.

You fill the spaces no one else can see,
And in your love,
Norisha found all she could be.

(27)

Closing Note

To all the dogs
who've touched our hearts,
You are the keepers of joy,
love, and art.

In you, we find home, through every storm—
You are our constant, our warm.

Forever, and always, we'll hold you near,
In the heart of a dog, you'll always be here.

— With love, Norisha Taylor

Dear Readers,

As you turn this last page, may the love, joy, and memories of dogs past and present stay close to your heart. These poems were written to honor the unbreakable bond between humans and their canine companions—a love that speaks in wagging tails, warm gazes, and silent understanding.

If this book touched your heart, made you smile, or brought back cherished memories, I would love to hear from you! Your thoughts and reviews help share this celebration of dogs with others who hold them dear.

📌 **Share Your Love & Feedback**
Scan the code below to leave a review—it only takes a moment but means the world. Your words can help another dog lover find comfort and joy in these pages.

To leave a review, scan the QR code provided and it will not take more than 2 minutes to leave your review.

Amazon.com	Amazon.in	Amazon.co.uk	Amazon.ca

🌐 www.ujbbooks.com
f www.facebook.com/ujbbooks
📷 www.instagram.com/ujbbooks
✉ editor@ujbbooks.com

Check out our other books Available on Amazon

Printed in Dunstable, United Kingdom